DATE DUE

PRAIRIE GIRL

The Life of

LAURA

INGALLS

WILDER

By William Anderson

Illustrations by Renée Graef

HarperCollins*Publishers*

Library of Congress Cataloging-in-Publication Data
Anderson, William, date
Prairie girl : the life of Laura Ingalls Wilder / by William Anderson ;
illustrations by Renée Graef.— 1st ed.   p.   cm.
Summary: A biography of Laura Ingalls Wilder, author of the "Little House"
books, from her Wisconsin childhood until her death at the age of ninety.
ISBN 0-06-028973-2 — ISBN 0-06-028974-0 (lib. bdg.)
1. Wilder, Laura Ingalls, 1867–1957—Juvenile literature. 2. Authors,
American—20th century—Biography—Juvenile literature. 3. Frontier and
pioneer life—United States—Juvenile literature. 4. Children's stories—
Authorship—Juvenile literature. [1. Wilder, Laura Ingalls, 1867–1957. 2.
Authors, American. 3. Women—Biography.] I. Graef, Renée, ill. II. Title.
PS3545.I342Z5635 2004   2003004444   813'.52—dc21   CIP   AC

Typography by Carla Weise
3 4 5 6 7 8 9 10
❖
First Edition

Contents

Chapter One

Log Cabin in the Woods

AFTER SUPPER, when the sky grew dark and flames danced in the fireplace inside the little log cabin, Laura Ingalls would ask, "Pa, will you please play the fiddle?"

The jolly songs Pa played on his fiddle made Laura want to dance and sing. Mary, Laura's older sister, loved Pa's music too, and so did Ma, their quiet, gentle mother. While they all listened, their big bulldog, Jack, dozed in the doorway.

Too soon, Laura would hear the clock strike the hour of eight.

"Goodness, Charles," Ma would say. "It is time these children were asleep."

As Ma tucked the girls under the cozy quilts, Pa would play just one more song, his blue eyes twinkling.

Laura and her family lived during the pioneer days of America. This was a time when many Americans left the East to find new homes in the West. When Laura was growing up during the 1860s and early 1870s, there were no telephones or electric lights. Most people traveled by horse and wagon. Many families like Laura's lived in log cabins. Pa had built their cabin in the big woods of Wisconsin, and it was the first home Laura remembered. Pa and Ma came there to live soon after their marriage in 1860. Mary was born in the log cabin in the woods in 1865, the year the Civil War ended. Laura was born there two years later, on February 7, 1867.

By 1868, Pa and Ma had decided to leave the cabin in the woods in search of a new home. The Wisconsin woods were filling up with new

settlers, and as hunting and trapping increased, wild animals became scarce. Pa knew that west of the Mississippi River lay vast stretches of open prairie, and that was where he wanted to go.

Pa sang a song with his fiddle that went "Uncle Sam is rich enough to give us all a farm." Laura knew her uncles Henry and Tom and Peter and George, but she did not know an Uncle Sam. Pa told Laura that Uncle Sam was really the United States government. The government had so much land to spare that it would give Pa a farm just for settling on the land. Pa said this was called homesteading.

The family traveled by covered wagon across Minnesota, Iowa, Missouri, and finally into Kansas. After many weeks of travel, they drove through the frontier town of Independence and continued on for a few more miles until Pa decided to stop. There was nothing around them except for the sea of tall prairie grass waving in the wind and a big blue bowl of sky overhead.

The family's first priority was to build a

house. Pa cut trees from creek banks nearby and built a one-room log cabin. Then he built a stable for the horses. Next he plowed up the prairie land and planted crops and a garden, and he dug a well for fresh water.

There were only a few settlers living near the Ingalls cabin. Most of the neighbors were Osage Indians. They lived in big camps because this was their territory. The government had moved them to Kansas many years before, when pioneers crowded their hunting grounds in Missouri. Osage tribesmen rode their ponies across the prairie and sometimes stopped at the cabin. They always seemed hungry and welcomed the corn bread Ma gave them.

On a hot day in August, Pa took Laura and Mary on a long walk across the prairie. Jack followed them. Laura was just three and a half, but she never forgot that day. The Indians were away hunting, and Pa wanted to show Laura and Mary their empty camp. For part of the walk across the prairie, Laura rode on Jack's broad back. At the camp they saw holes in the ground where tent poles had been and black spots where campfires had burned. In the dust Laura and Mary spied colored beads. They hunted for those left-behind beads until each had a handful.

When they arrived home, there was a surprise better than beads. A neighbor woman had come over to visit with Ma before they left, and now there was a third person in the cabin—a tiny newborn baby wrapped in a quilt. Laura looked at the little red-faced baby who snuggled next to Ma. Ma told Mary and Laura that this was their new sister, Caroline, whom they would call Carrie. In the family Bible, Ma wrote Carrie's birthdate: August 3, 1870.

Soon after baby Carrie was born, the prairie became less peaceful. Laura heard Indian war cries during the night. The Osages were unhappy that people like the Ingallses had settled on their land. The Osages had agreed to sell their land, but the American government in Washington had not yet paid them for their territory. Night after night, the Indians chanted in their camps and debated what to do. Their angry cries floated across the prairie and frightened Laura, even though Pa was nearby and Jack guarded the cabin door.

When a treaty with the Indians was finally settled, the Osage tribe left the prairie. Laura watched with Ma and Pa and Mary as a long line of Osage men, women, and children on foot and on horseback moved to another reservation farther west.

Not long afterward, Pa and Ma received a letter from Wisconsin. The man who had bought their farm could not pay and wanted Pa to take it back. Even though the prairie was now peaceful, Pa and Ma decided to leave. They traveled all the way back home to Wisconsin, to the house where Mary and Laura had been born. Although Laura was only four years old, she never forgot Kansas, and Pa and Ma and Mary always told her stories of their first travels.

Back in Wisconsin, the cabin was shaded by tall trees instead of wide, open prairie skies.

When Laura looked out the window, she saw more trees, leading to the deep forest. Inside the house were familiar things that had traveled back with them from Kansas: Pa's fiddle, the chiming clock, the colorful quilts, and Ma's precious little china figure, a shepherdess.

In the big woods Pa had many jobs to do each day. During the winter, when drifts of snow filled the silent forest, Pa left the warm house to hunt and check his traps. He brought home deer meat and sometimes bear meat. The animals he trapped were valuable for their silky furs. Pa collected them all winter. Then he traded them at the store in Pepin, seven miles away. It was the town closest to the Ingalls cabin.

Laura missed Pa terribly when he made the long trip to Pepin, but she was excited when he returned, bringing things they could not produce on their farm, such as sugar, salt, and spices. He also brought kerosene for the lamp, and sometimes there were lengths of cloth for Ma to make clothes. Laura and Mary always waited impatiently while Pa unpacked his purchases. They knew Pa would also have a treat for them, perhaps a stick of peppermint candy!

In the spring Pa cleared away trees surrounding the cabin. In the open spaces he raised wheat and corn. A garden provided vegetables and fruits for the family. A cow and a calf lived in the log barn. Pa built a zigzag rail fence to protect everything from the wild animals that roamed the woods. In cold weather he chopped wood to feed the stove and the fireplace.

While Pa worked outside, Ma, Laura, and Mary were busy in the cabin. By the time Laura was five, she knew that each day had its own job. She and Mary helped Ma wash clothes on Mondays. On Tuesdays Ma ironed, and Wednesdays were for sewing. On Thursdays they churned butter, and on Fridays they cleaned the cabin. Laura loved Saturdays because they were baking days, and the whole cabin was filled with the warm, yeasty smell of bread. And every day Ma cooked breakfast, dinner, and supper on the black iron cookstove.

On Sundays Mary and Laura dressed in their best clothes and wore hair ribbons in their braids. They sat quietly while Ma read Bible stories aloud. Sundays were God's day, so everyone must be extra quiet and extra good. It seemed to Laura that Mary was *always* well behaved. She sat so ladylike while Laura felt like running and talking and playing with Jack. She felt better listening to Pa play his fiddle. On Sundays he played and sang songs like "Sweet Sabbath Home," "Rock of Ages," and "In the Sweet By and By."

Ma expected Laura and Mary to learn to sew because all of their clothes were made at home. Mary made a whole patchwork quilt by the time she was five. Laura hated sewing. She thought it was slow and boring work, but she learned because Ma wanted her to. She was proud when she finished sewing her first sampler. On a length of gray cloth she sewed sample stitches with red yarn.

Laura was happiest when she was outdoors.

Each day she brought in chips from the woodpile by the cabin door. The wood chips helped start fires in the stove and fireplace. Laura worked hard at her job, though she was very small. She was so short that Pa called her half-pint. He said she was like a pint of cider, half drunk up!

Down the twisting path from the cabin was a school. Ma told Laura and Mary that she had been a teacher and that schools were special places. Both Pa and Ma loved books, and many nights Laura fell asleep hearing Ma read. Ma said Laura would learn to read all by herself in school.

Laura and Mary walked to school together and carried their lunch in a dinner pail. At five years old, Laura was one of the youngest pupils in the school. She learned to print letters and discovered that letters made whole words. Laura was excited when she could read her first words:

The sun is up and it is day.
The dew is on the new-mown hay.

At recess time all the children in the school played together. Mary walked and talked quietly with the older girls, but Laura ran and jumped and climbed trees. When recess was over, Laura returned to the schoolroom with her dress rumpled and her brown braids flying.

After two years in the big woods, Pa and Ma discussed another move west. Pa said that Wisconsin was too crowded. New houses and farms were being built, and the forest was being cleared away. Pa missed the hunting and the big open prairies of Kansas.

Ma was happy living in their cabin in the woods, but she agreed with Pa. They could find a better farm in the West. Across the Mississippi River was a big state called Minnesota. In the western part of the state, the hills and valleys flattened out into prairie land. That was where Pa wanted to homestead.

Chapter Two

Pioneering on Plum Creek

 ONE WINTER MORNING Laura woke up and saw that the cabin was nearly empty. Pa and Ma had packed most of their belongings in the canvas-topped wagon that waited in the yard. Quilts and bedding nearly filled the wagon, along with dishes and clothing and the clock. Pa's fiddle rested between the quilts so that it would ride safely. Pa hooked his gun near the wagon seat for protection.

Pa had sold the cabin and the cow. Heavy furniture was left behind because the wagon could not be too heavy for the horses to pull on the long journey west. Pa hoisted Mary and Laura and baby Carrie into the wagon, and they nestled on a pile of quilts. Ma and Pa sat on the seat ahead while Jack walked behind the wagon.

Leaving their cabin behind for the second time, Pa drove the wagon through the wintry woods. They spent the first night of their trip west in a hotel. It was February 7, 1874, Laura's seventh birthday. Pa and Ma surprised her with a book of poems called *The Floweret*.

Pa wanted to settle in the western part of Minnesota, but the weather was too cold to drive that far in the wagon. Pa found a cabin where they could wait until springtime. When warm weather came, their journey continued. Each day Pa drove the horses and wagon fifteen to twenty miles farther west. The land grew flatter the farther they traveled.

Each day as the sun set in the west, Pa stopped at a camping spot. Then there was work to do. Pa tended the tired horses and built a campfire. He hunted for fat prairie chickens and rabbits. Ma mixed batter for corn bread, and Mary and Laura opened the dish box. The supper table was a clean cloth spread on the grass.

As the big prairie sky grew dark with night, the campfire burned cheerily. It shed a warm glow on Laura and her family. Before bedtime Pa played the fiddle. Laura liked the going-somewhere songs Pa played.

"Oh Susanna, don't you cry for me," Pa sang along with the fiddle. And this song seemed just right for pioneers going west:

In the starlight, in the starlight let us
wander gay and free,
For there's nothing in the daylight half
so dear to you and me.

Laura and her sisters went to sleep in the wagon while Pa sang his songs over the wide, dark prairie of Minnesota.

One day as the covered wagon jolted along the road west, Laura saw something unusual. It was a locomotive, speeding across the prairie. It traveled much faster than Pa's horses could pull the wagon. Pa told Laura it was a train and that it was the fastest way to travel. Laura never forgot the sight of that sleek train with plumes of black smoke pouring from the engine's smokestack.

After stopping in a village called Walnut Grove, Pa drove the wagon out on the prairie and stopped, announcing they were home. Laura saw no house, no well for water, and no stable for the horses. There was just grass and sky and a creek bank with a stream of shining water called Plum Creek.

But there *was* a house, a house like none they had ever seen. It was a dugout, hollowed into the side of the creek bank. The floor was earth, and the front wall was built of lengths of grassy sod, piled up like bricks. Even the roof was made of strips of sod held up by wooden logs. Wild grasses and flowers grew on the outside walls. Trees were few on the prairie, and dugout houses were common. Laura liked the little sod house. At night the sound of the creek sang her to sleep, and in the morning it called her to the door.

While Pa plowed up the prairie for a wheat field, Laura, Mary, and Carrie helped Ma turn the dugout into a home. Laura fetched pails of water from the running spring. She and Mary played with little Carrie and made sure she did not fall into Plum Creek. When plums ripened, Laura and Mary picked them for Ma. Laura fished and brought strings of her catch to Ma to cook.

Plum Creek was Laura's playground. She never tired of splashing, wading, and playing with Jack in the creek. Mary sometimes joined her, but often she was in the dugout with Ma or sewing quietly on a patchwork quilt.

After Pa had planted his wheat crop, he had time to build a better house for the family. He hauled lumber and doors and windows from Walnut Grove and built a beautiful, roomy home not far from the dugout on the prairie. It had a big room for cooking and eating. A smaller room was Pa and Ma's bedroom. A ladder led to the attic, which was an airy bedroom for Laura and

Mary. Carrie slept downstairs until she was old enough to climb the ladder to the attic safely.

After they were settled in the new house, Ma surprised Laura and Mary. She said they could walk to school in Walnut Grove since it was just a mile from Plum Creek.

Laura was shy on the first day she and Mary arrived at school. She knew none of the children, and she felt bashful. Being with Mary helped. Laura practiced writing on her shiny, new black slate. Words excited her—both reading them and writing them. And Laura quickly learned her classmates' names and forgot about being shy.

School became great fun for Laura, especially at recess. Everyone wanted Laura to play games, even the boys. She could run as fast as anyone in the school and was popular with all of her classmates.

While Mary and Laura were at school, Pa worked hard along Plum Creek. He bought a cow and built a stable. Every day the wheat grew taller. Pa explained that folks in big cities

like St. Paul needed wheat to make flour. When Pa's crop was harvested, he could sell it in Walnut Grove. He told Laura that the wheat would make them rich.

But Pa had no chance to sell his wheat. One terrible day in the summer of 1875, the sky darkened with strange clouds. Instead of rain, big green grasshoppers plopped on the ground. They ate Pa's wheat field. They ate the garden. They ate the grass Pa's cow needed. They ate everything that was green, leaving the Minnesota prairie brown and bare.

Laura had never seen Pa so disappointed. Even his blue eyes looked sad. The wheat crop had meant money in Pa's pocket. It would have paid for the new house and bought shoes and dresses and food from the store. Without the crop, Pa needed to work for wages. There were no jobs nearby, so he had to leave home to search for work. Pa walked more than a hundred miles before he found a job harvesting wheat that the grasshoppers hadn't eaten.

While Pa was gone, Laura worked harder

than she ever had, helping Ma with Pa's chores. Being busy didn't keep them from missing Pa. The house on Plum Creek seemed empty without his jolly songs, his twinkling eyes, and his happy fiddle playing.

Letters came from Pa and helped to lift their spirits. Finally when harvesting was finished, he walked home to Plum Creek. He arrived with his pockets full of money, whistling "When Johnny Comes Marching Home Again."

Chapter Three

Back-Trailers
to Iowa

SOON AFTER PA CAME HOME, Laura and Mary returned from school to find that there was another Charles in the house! Charles Frederick was born on November 1, 1875. The family called the baby Freddie.

The next year was America's centennial birthday, but no one in Walnut Grove was celebrating in 1876. The prairie was dry and brown, and farmers like Pa could grow no crops. Grasshoppers were still in abundance, searching for something to eat. One family saw them trying to eat the paint from their house. People abandoned their farms and homes. Laura said good-bye to many of her friends at school. And then Pa told them that they would leave too.

Laura didn't like to think of her family leaving the West and returning to the East. People who did that were called back-trailers. Pa and Laura loved the West more than anyone in their family. But Pa had to earn money. The Steadmans, a Walnut Grove family, had bought a hotel in Burr Oak, Iowa. They needed help operating the hotel, so Pa and Ma agreed to move with their family to Burr Oak. They planned to live in the hotel and share the work.

Laura was nine, and Pa told her she was as strong as a little French horse. She helped pack the wagon while Mary tended Freddie and kept track of five-year-old Carrie. When the Ingalls family left Walnut Grove, Laura wondered if she would ever see it again.

On the trip to Iowa, the Ingallses stopped to visit Uncle Peter and Aunt Eliza and their children, who had lived near them in the big woods. Uncle Peter invited Laura's family to visit for several weeks in eastern Minnesota. The cousins spent the long summer days playing together and helping with the chores.

During the visit at Uncle Peter's, nine-month-old Freddie was sick. Pa and Ma did all they could to help him, but at the end of August Freddie died. He was buried near Uncle Peter's farm. When the time came for the Ingalls family to leave for Iowa, they sadly left Freddie behind in his little grave.

As the wagon headed toward Iowa, Pa and Ma and Mary and Laura and Carrie mourned for the baby. Laura remembered Ma saying, "Always be happy with what you have." She was grateful she still had Pa and Ma and Mary and Carrie.

Laura loved Pa for his fiddling and stories. She loved Ma for being so calm and patient and loving. And Carrie and Mary were her best friends. Though Mary was so perfect and so smart that Laura was sometimes jealous, she admired her. Once she wrote a poem just for Mary:

Who is it trusts me
without doubt
And ere she knows what
I'm about?
Who will come quickly
to help me out?
My sister Mary

Mary and Laura wondered what Burr Oak would be like. Pa told them it was an old town, not a prairie settlement like Walnut Grove. When the wagon finally arrived in Burr Oak, Laura saw brick houses standing solid on the hills. Stores and houses and a church stood close together on a winding street. Pa stopped the horses in front of a big, wooden hotel. Laura saw lamplight from the windows, and from the front doors came sounds of people laughing and chattering and smells of supper cooking. Other wagons stood in the yard of the hotel.

Laura had never lived among so many people. Her family crowded in with the Steadmans,

25

who owned the hotel, and all the people who stayed there. Laura and Mary were very busy. They helped with the hotel work, especially with the piles of dishes to wash.

Laura and Mary and Carrie attended the redbrick Burr Oak school. Laura was excited about learning how to spell more words and read books. She memorized and recited long poems. Arithmetic was not her favorite subject, but Laura learned the multiplication tables by singing them along with the class.

Pa and Ma soon realized that the hotel was no place for their family. It was too noisy and crowded. They found a brick house to rent on the edge of town and were happy to live alone once more. In May 1877 a new baby was born there, a blue-eyed sister named Grace. That summer ten-year-old Laura had two chores: fetching the cows from their pasture and helping Ma with Grace.

Pa worked hard at several jobs in Burr Oak, but it seemed there was never enough money to support their family of six. One day a lady in

Burr Oak named Mrs. Starr came visiting and asked Ma if she might adopt Laura. The Starr children were all grown, and Mrs. Starr was lonely. She thought she could help out the large Ingalls family by taking one of their children. Laura was horrified! She was relieved when she heard Ma refuse Mrs. Starr gently, saying, "Mr. Ingalls and I couldn't possibly spare Laura!"

Laura longed to go west again, and in 1878 she and her family did. They left Burr Oak behind and returned to Walnut Grove. How Laura enjoyed traveling in the covered wagon! She couldn't decide what was best: mornings, with the beautiful sunrise at their backs, or driving into the setting sun in the evening while they searched for a camping spot.

Back in Walnut Grove, Pa built a little house in the middle of a meadow in town. Pa had sold the farm on Plum Creek, so Laura and Mary and Carrie were now town girls. They returned to the Walnut Grove school, and every Sunday they went to the Congregational church with Pa and Ma. School, church, and chores kept Laura very busy.

Mary worried that Laura was a tomboy, because at recess she ran as fast as the rowdy boys and even beat them at baseball. When Mary told Ma how wild Laura was, Laura couldn't resist: She stuck her tongue out at Mary and called her a tattletale!

Although Laura could be a tomboy, she was also very responsible. She was eleven when she got her first job. Mrs. Masters, who ran the Walnut Grove hotel, asked Laura to help. Again Laura was busy in a hotel, washing dishes and setting tables. Her favorite job was arranging spoons in a holder, just like a bouquet. Each week Laura earned fifty cents, which she gave to Ma.

Laura turned twelve in the winter of 1879. Snow and blizzard winds kept Pa at home, so he took out his fiddle and played dance music. Pa and Ma taught Laura and Carrie to waltz and polka. When they had learned the steps, they sailed around and around the room, dancing to the music of the fiddle.

In the spring of 1879, Mary became very sick. The doctor said that Mary had brain fever, which was very serious. Her fever was so high that all of her lovely long blond hair was cut short to cool her. Mary finally began to recover, but the sight in her eyes had faded. Mary was blind.

Laura knew how important it was when Pa told her that she must serve as Mary's eyes. Her duty was to tell Mary what happened around her. She started immediately, describing to Mary everything she saw: clouds, sunsets, people, and places. Laura hoped her words would help Mary imagine the things she could no longer see.

Chapter Four

Homesteading in Dakota

PA LEFT WALNUT GROVE in the summer
of 1879 to take a job with the railroad
company that was building tracks west into
Dakota Territory. Pa's job was to keep track of
the workers' wages and pay them. He wanted to
move west, but he needed money to start farming again. The railroad job paid him fifty dollars
a month, which he carefully saved.

Laura knew that Pa was looking for a homestead. Ma agreed that it would be nice to farm
again, but she also asked Pa to promise that
going to Dakota was their last move. Pa agreed;

he was eager to get another chance at Uncle Sam's land.

Laura helped Ma pack some of their belongings for the move, and they sold the rest. Laura was surprised when Ma told her they would make part of the journey on the railroad. They had never traveled by train. All in a morning, the swift train took them to Tracy, Minnesota.

Pa met his family where the railroad tracks ended in Tracy. They traveled on by wagon across the prairie to the Silver Lake railroad camp where Pa worked. The family lived in a tiny shanty near the lake. The one-room shanty was the smallest house Laura had ever lived in and was built with only a single thickness of pine lumber. From the doorway, Laura saw in the distance clouds of dust and plows and scrapers and horses and men. Everyone was hurrying to finish the railroad before snow and cold weather arrived.

When the Silver Lake camp closed for the winter, Pa was offered a new job. The railroad company asked him to stay behind and guard the camp. The surveyors who measured out the railroad tracks wanted to go back east for the winter. Their roomy, comfortable house at the edge of the lake was empty, and the Ingalls family could move in. It was full of food and fuel, enough to last until spring.

Laura was excited that they could stay in Dakota Territory. Now that all the workers were gone for the winter, the prairie was empty. There were no neighbors for miles around. Best of all, Pa found a homestead he liked on the other side of Silver Lake, just a mile from where a town would be built in the spring.

The Ingalls family had a cozy winter on Silver Lake. Laura and Carrie slid on the ice and played in the snow. Pa fiddled in the warm house. Laura read stories aloud so that Mary could enjoy them. They feasted on supplies left in the surveyors' pantry. There were sacks of beans and potatoes, barrels of flour and cornmeal, and even some canned pickles and peaches.

When the snow melted, homesteaders flocked into Dakota to stake their land claims. All over the empty prairie, men claimed land where they would build houses and farms. Pa said they were living in the Dakota land rush. Suddenly a new town named De Smet appeared. Laura's quiet prairie was gone.

Laura was happier when Pa moved them to his homestead claim, a mile from De Smet. He quickly built a tiny shanty, and they squeezed everything inside. Pa planned to add rooms to the little house when he had more time and money. There was so much to do on the homestead that thirteen-year-old Laura was Pa's helper once again. They built a stable and planted a garden. All summer Laura helped Pa cut and stack prairie grass for hay. Hay could be sold, and it was needed to feed Pa's horses and the family's new cow.

Laura worked so hard that summer that sometimes her legs and back ached. But she never complained. One evening in the flickering lamplight, she wrote:

If you've anything to do
Do it with all your might.
Don't let trifles hinder you
If you're sure you're right.
Work away, work away,
Do it with all your might.

In October 1880, soon after Laura and Pa had cut and stacked the last of the hay, a blizzard swept over the prairie. Pa knew they could not survive in the thin-walled shanty through the winter. He had built a store to rent out along Main Street in De Smet, and it stood empty. Quickly Pa moved the family to his building in town. Then the blizzards started blowing regularly.

For a while Laura and Carrie attended the first school in De Smet. Soon even going to school became too dangerous. No one knew when a blizzard would hit and strand the children in the schoolhouse, which was just three blocks from Main Street. Snowdrifts mounted, and trains from the East carrying supplies were blocked. De Smet quickly ran out of food and coal.

Blizzards often lasted two or three days. While the fierce winds blew, it was not safe to leave the house. The snow was so thick that Laura could see only a white blur outside the window. During the blizzards everyone sat close to the stove, huddled in quilts and shawls. Throughout the long hours Ma read aloud, Pa played the fiddle, and they often sang to drown out the sounds of the raging wind. They went to bed early to save fuel and kerosene for the lamp.

By January 1881, the family had little left to eat. They had eaten all the potatoes. The flour sack was empty. Sugar was gone. Then Pa brought in a sack of wheat from the Wilder brothers' feed store. Laura helped grind the wheat into flour, and every day Ma baked a loaf of brown bread. For each meal they ate bread and drank hot tea.

The coal was also gone, so between blizzards Pa hauled in the hay he and Laura had cut from the homestead. Pa showed Laura how to twist strands of hay into sticks to use as fuel. She and

Pa twisted hay constantly to keep the stove warm. Still, the house was never very warm because the temperature outside was often forty below zero.

On days when the blizzard winds died down, Pa visited the stores along Main Street. He learned that all of De Smet was cold and hungry, and there was no wheat left for anyone.

In February two young men, Cap Garland and Almanzo Wilder, went in search of wheat that was rumored to be stored in a homesteader's shanty. The rumor was true. They bought it all and hauled it back to town just before another blizzard struck. Each family in De Smet bought enough wheat to survive until spring.

The blizzards finally stopped in April. Slowly the huge snowdrifts melted, and everyone waited for the first supply train to arrive.

When Laura heard the whistle of the train bringing food and supplies, she knew that she had helped her family survive the worst winter they had ever known, and she had learned how powerful nature could be.

Chapter Five

Laura, Manly, and Rose

AFTER THE LONG, HARD WINTER, Pa and Ma enrolled Mary in a college for blind students in Vinton, Iowa. Pa and Ma traveled with Mary by train to settle her in the school. There Mary was taught Braille, studied music, and learned crafts. Every evening as Laura studied her lessons at home, she imagined Mary, far away, doing the same.

Laura became the best student in the De Smet school. She studied reading, geography, spelling, arithmetic, history, and writing. She also had fun with her classmates. She was still shy, but she went skating and attended parties. Laura wanted to be fashionable, and she earned money for clothes by sewing for the dressmaker in De Smet.

In De Smet the finest team of horses was driven by Almanzo Wilder, one of the young homesteaders who had gone in search of wheat the previous winter. Each time she saw them, Laura wished she might ride behind those horses. One day at church, Laura was surprised when Almanzo asked if he could walk her home. Laura was so tongue-tied, she could hardly speak as they walked together. He told her he was from New York State, but he had a homestead north of De Smet.

Soon after Laura met Almanzo, she passed a teacher's examination and was asked to teach for two months at a school twelve miles from De Smet. Laura hadn't expected to teach so soon, but the school offered her twenty dollars a month in wages. Even though she did not want to leave home to teach, she knew that her earnings would help keep Mary in college.

The Bouchie school was in an abandoned shanty sitting alone on the white, snow-covered prairie. When Laura met her five pupils, she discovered that two of them were older than she was. She wondered if she could teach them all. But Laura quickly organized the little school into classes and assigned lessons.

Laura's first week teaching at the Bouchie school was lonely. She lived with Mr. and Mrs. Bouchie in their shanty near the school. Each evening Laura continued studying her own lessons, but she missed Pa and Ma and her sisters. On Friday of her first week as a teacher, Laura dreaded spending the weekend so far from home.

Just as Laura dismissed her students on Friday, she heard sleigh bells jingling across the snowy prairie. Almanzo, whom Laura now called Manly, had arrived in his cutter to drive her home for the weekend!

Each Friday Manly drove Laura home. Every Sunday he returned her to the Bouchies. Each week Laura grew more confident teaching. She

was always homesick, but her students liked her and she liked them. They were sorry when the term ended and Laura returned to De Smet and became a student once again.

In the spring Manly asked Laura to go buggy riding with him on the prairie. All summer they took long rides together across the prairie, with the tall grasses and wild red roses swishing against the black buggy wheels. Laura discovered that she liked Manly better than any of the boys she knew in De Smet.

Laura taught at a second school the next year, this time just a short walk from home. Manly continued visiting, and he took Laura to dances and socials and to a singing school at the church. He told Laura about his homestead land, his crops, and the house he planned to build on the prairie. Manly asked Laura to marry him and Laura said yes. After Laura and Manly were engaged, she taught at one more school. She was eighteen and felt very grown up, teaching at her third school and wearing a shiny engagement ring.

On August 25, 1885, Laura and Manly were married. Laura had asked to remove the word "obey" from the wedding ceremony. She later wrote, "We started even each alike promising to love, honor and respect the other." Laura and Manly ate a wedding dinner with Pa and Ma and Carrie and Grace. Then it was time for Laura to leave for her new home with Manly.

On his homestead tree claim a mile from De Smet was the prettiest little gray house she had ever seen. Manly had built it for their new life together. The house had three rooms: a sitting room, a bedroom, and a kitchen with a pantry. Through the windows Laura could see miles and miles of rolling green prairie land and blue sky. Beyond the house were ten acres of little trees that Manly had planted to provide shade and to break the wind. Past the trees were fields of ripening grain. Laura and Manly discussed plans for the farm, and they decided that they would be equal partners in the business of wheat farming.

In June 1886 it seemed that all of Dakota

Territory was covered with wild roses. Manly drove Laura over the prairie to admire the pink blossoms. On the drive Laura told Manly that she was expecting a baby. Manly wondered about a name for their child. Laura was certain that the child would be a girl, and she wanted to call her Rose. Laura was right. On December 5, 1886, a pretty, blue-eyed girl was born and they named her Rose.

All through the winter Laura and Manly watched their Rose grow big and healthy. They wrapped her well and took her sleigh riding to see Pa and Ma. Pa had given up his homestead and built a house in De Smet for the family. He became De Smet's carpenter, declaring that his farming days were finished.

It seemed to Laura that farming brought nothing but misfortunes in the years after Rose was born. Manly worked hard, but in 1887 the drought years in Dakota began. Hail leveled their wheat fields. They could not pay their debts. Laura worried and wondered if they should give up homesteading.

Then Laura and Manly became very ill with diphtheria, a contagious respiratory disease. Rose was safe with Pa and Ma during the weeks they recovered. Manly's strength was slow to return. He shuffled through his chores, and often Laura left her work in the house to help him in the barn and in the fields.

In 1889 they had their saddest year. A baby son was born in August, but two weeks later he died suddenly. One day soon after, Laura heard the crackling sound of fire. Hay had caught fire near the cookstove, and the kitchen was ablaze. Laura grabbed Rose and rushed out onto the prairie. The little gray house burned, and only a black hole remained.

After the fire Laura and Manly became wanderers. They traveled with Rose to Minnesota to spend the summer with Manly's parents. Manly was still weak from his illness, so they took the train to the panhandle of Florida, thinking the warm weather would help. It didn't seem to do any good, so after a year they returned to De Smet.

De Smet was still suffering from drought. Instead of farming, Laura and Manly rented a house in town, close to Pa and Ma's new home. Manly worked when he could, and Laura took a job sewing at the dressmaker's. At the age of five, Rose started school.

Laura earned a dollar a day from her sewing. She saved the money because she and Manly had a plan. They still wanted to farm, but not in dusty, dry Dakota. They had heard of new farming country among the green hills of the Ozark Mountains in Missouri, called the Land of the Big Red Apple.

In the summer of 1894, Laura and Manly were ready to leave South Dakota and move to Missouri.

Chapter Six

Pioneering
in the Ozarks

EARLY ON THE MORNING of July 17, 1894, Laura and Manly and Rose said good-bye to Pa and Ma and Mary and Carrie and Grace. They left De Smet in a covered wagon and headed south.

For a month the Wilders drove through South Dakota, Nebraska, and Kansas. Each night they camped in a new spot, and Laura cooked over a campfire. She told Rose they were on one long picnic.

As the wagon jolted and creaked along the roads, Laura kept a diary. She thought it would be interesting to read about the trip sometime in the future. She wrote about the towns they passed, the people they met, and the farms they saw. She described the stormy crossing they made on the Missouri River as they left South Dakota and arrived in Nebraska. She wrote of wading with Rose in creeks and feasting on watermelons and other fruit they bought along the way.

On the afternoon of August 22, Laura recorded in her diary that they crossed the Missouri state line. As the wagon rolled on, Laura saw healthy green crops; springs of clear, cold water; and beautiful forests. Blue hazy hills and rocky-edged ravines appeared.

Laura told Rose that this was the Ozark country. They were so glad to be in Missouri that they sang "Ta-rah-rah-BOOM-de-ay" as they neared the town of Mansfield.

As Manly drove the wagon around a bend into Mansfield, Laura said that this was where they would stop.

With a hundred-dollar bill Laura had saved from her sewing job in De Smet, she and Manly bought a farm a mile from Mansfield. The forty acres of land needed work; it was rocky and covered by timber and brush. But Laura loved the new land. She was sure it could be transformed into a beautiful home. Not long after the Wilders moved into the log cabin that stood on their own hilltop, Laura named the place Rocky Ridge Farm.

Laura and Rose cleaned the empty cabin and made it homelike with the belongings they had brought from De Smet. The cabin reminded Laura of her log home in the big woods of Wisconsin when she was a little girl.

When they were settled, Laura sent Rose down the road to the Mansfield school. Already, at the age of seven, Rose showed signs of loving words and stories and ideas, just as Laura had. She read all the books she could find and quickly became a top scholar at school.

Laura helped Manly clear their land. She enjoyed working in the woods, pulling one end of the crosscut saw as they cleared space for fields and pastures. Together Laura and Manly

carefully planted four hundred little apple trees on their land.

Slowly Rocky Ridge became a farm. Cattle grazed on the hills. Corn grew in the cleared fields. The fruit trees started bearing. Laura and Manly shipped apples and pears and grapes and berries for city people to enjoy.

Laura worked hard, but she knew that hard work never hurt anyone. She tended the vegetable garden, churned butter, baked bread, and raised chickens. She sewed Manly's shirts and made dresses for herself and Rose. From sunrise to sunset each day, Laura was busy.

When chores were finished, Laura found time for fun. She and Rose played in the creek behind the cabin. They tamed wild birds and animals. Rose's school friends came to explore the woods that covered much of Rocky Ridge Farm.

On Sundays Manly took the family buggy riding. Laura packed picnic lunches, and they ate under the tall trees. In the evenings at home, Laura read aloud to Manly and Rose from *The*

Youth's Companion. Rose borrowed books from the school library, and Laura read them by the light of the kerosene lamp. While Laura read, Manly made popcorn for a treat.

After a few years of living on the farm and then in a little house in Mansfield, Laura drew plans for a new farmhouse. She believed that a house in the country should be built from materials from the land. Manly cut down huge oak trees from Rocky Ridge. He hauled them to the sawmill and brought back great timbers and boards for building. He and Laura collected stones from the fields for the foundation and fireplace.

Laura wanted wide, broad windows of clear glass so that she could look out onto the fields and woods. She planned three porches so she could always find a cool place on hot days. She loved to read, so a corner of the parlor was set aside for a little library. Laura loved fires crackling on a hearth, so a mammoth rock fireplace was planned for one end of the parlor.

The house on Rocky Ridge was started in

1896. Slowly but steadily, Laura saw her house expand. Rooms and improvements were added until finally there were ten rooms. It took nearly seventeen years to finish the house. When it was done, people from all around the countryside called the Wilder house one of the prettiest places in the Ozarks. Rocky Ridge Farm grew too. Laura and Manly saved money and continued to buy more land until they owned nearly two hundred acres.

In 1903 Rose finished high school. After graduation, Rose learned telegraphy at the railroad depot in Mansfield. Tapping out messages on the telegraph key was the fastest means of communication in America, and it was one of the few jobs open to women. Soon Rose was offered a telegraphy job in Kansas City.

Rose was seventeen when she left home to work. Women all over were becoming "career girls," and Rose was eager to live and work in Kansas City. Her first job paid her sixty dollars a month, which was enough to support herself. Laura sometimes worried about Rose living so far from Rocky Ridge. Rose reminded her that she could board the train and arrive home in less than a day.

Laura marveled at the modern times she lived in. Fast trains, telephones, automobiles, and electric lights were all common in the town of Mansfield and were even spreading to the countryside. Laura knew that the time would come when people would forget what covered wagons were. But *she* would never forget the covered-wagon trips with Pa and Ma and her sisters, nor the journey with Manly and Rose to Rocky Ridge Farm.

Chapter Seven

Writing in Orange-Covered Tablets

AFTER LIVING FOR MANY YEARS on Rocky Ridge Farm, Laura thought that no one worked harder than a farmer's wife. She knew the waiting and hoping for good crops. She also knew what it was like to work from sunrise to sunset. She churned butter, canned fruits and vegetables, tended chickens, and helped Manly when he needed her.

Rose suggested that Laura and Manly sell the farm and move to a city. Laura reminded Rose how much she and Manly loved the land. They decided to stay on Rocky Ridge Farm.

"We who live in quiet places," Laura wrote, "have the opportunity to think our own thoughts and live our own lives."

In 1911 Laura was surprised when a newspaper editor contacted her. He knew about the success of Rocky Ridge Farm and wanted Laura to write about it for the *Missouri Ruralist*. The *Ruralist* was a weekly paper for farm families published in St. Louis and read all over Missouri.

Laura accepted the job, and she made time in her busy days to write. In her articles, she shared her experiences of running the farm with Manly. She also gave tips on raising chickens and interviewed her neighbors about their farms in the Ozarks.

Laura proudly sent Rose her columns from the *Missouri Ruralist*. Rose had moved to California, where she married Gillette Lane. She joined her husband in selling real estate near San Francisco. Then, in 1914, Rose started her own career as a writer. She became a popular newspaper reporter for the *San Francisco Bulletin*.

In 1915 Laura received an invitation from Rose she could not resist. Rose told her of the great world's fair in San Francisco and begged her mother to visit. Manly urged Laura to go; he would stay home to tend the farm. So Laura made her longest trip west, all by railroad. Seeing Rose's smiling face at the San Francisco train station was the beginning of two of the most exciting months in Laura's life.

In San Francisco Laura waded in the Pacific Ocean. She rode cable cars up and down the streets of the hilly city. She tried the food in Chinese and Italian restaurants. For days she wandered through the wonders of the world's fair.

Laura loved the fireworks and fountains and exhibits from foreign lands. She was amazed to see the flying machines and to be able to watch a moving picture at a theater built for four thousand people. But she was homesick for Manly when she toured the farming exhibits at the fair. She wrote him letters all about modern milking machines, canning factories, and food exhibits.

Then Laura got a writing assignment. The *Missouri Ruralist* asked her to write stories about the fair. Rose worked with Laura on her articles for the *Ruralist*. Laura was glad to have her help. "I do the housework so that she will have time to help me," Laura told Manly. Finally Laura returned to Rocky Ridge. For ten more years she published articles in newspapers and magazines.

In 1925 Rose came back to Rocky Ridge to spend time with Laura and Manly. She was now a famous author. Rose had traveled throughout Europe as a reporter. Her books and magazine stories were read all across America. But Rose had never forgotten the stories Laura told of life as a pioneer girl. She encouraged Laura to write down her memories.

Laura sat at her desk and opened an orange-covered tablet of paper. She wrote page after page of stories of her life with Pa and Ma and Mary and Carrie and Grace. Laura's memories slipped back to life in the big woods, to the prairies, to Plum Creek, and to De Smet.

Suddenly Laura realized, "To my surprise, I have discovered that I have led a very interesting life."

Laura shared the stories in the orange tablets with Rose. Rose said, "Put some meat on the bones!" Rose wanted Laura to add details, write descriptions of the people and places she mentioned, and tell additional stories.

So Laura wrote and rewrote, emphasizing stories that her father had told her. Laura's manuscript became *Little House in the Big Woods*, the story of her first memories of log cabin life in Wisconsin. Then Rose showed Laura's writings to an editor at Harper & Brothers, a large publishing company in New York. The children's department decided to publish the first book written by Laura Ingalls Wilder. When the book was published in 1932, Laura was sixty-five years old.

Little House in the Big Woods was immediately popular with the children who read it. Teachers and librarians and parents liked the book too. Grandparents were pleased that

Laura had written of frontier life so that modern children could know how they had lived.

"I thought that would end it," Laura said when her first book was published. "But what do you think? Children who read them wrote to me, begging for more. I was amazed!"

Laura decided to respond to the children who wanted more stories. She wrote a second book, but not about herself. She filled more orange-covered tablets with stories of a boy who loved horses and who grew up on a big farm in New York State. It was Manly's story, and Laura called the book *Farmer Boy*.

Still, the requests for more books arrived. Laura spent hours at her desk, remembering and writing. "I went as far back in my memory as I could and left my mind there," Laura explained. It brought "out of the dimness of the past things that were beyond my ordinary remembrance." Laura's third book was published in 1935. It was *Little House on the Prairie*, the adventure story of her family's life on the Kansas prairie.

Letters kept pouring in to Laura from her readers. When Manly brought her the piles of letters from the mailbox, they all seemed to say, "What happened next? Please tell us more!" Laura smiled and kept on writing. She was reminded of the days long ago when she had begged Pa for just one more story and just one more song on his fiddle.

Chapter Eight

The Children's Favorite

In 1937 Laura turned seventy. She was a pretty lady with snow-white hair and snapping blue eyes. That year her fourth book, *On the Banks of Plum Creek*, was published.

Manly was just as surprised as Laura was that children liked the stories of their lives so much. But he left the writing to Laura and kept busy on the farm. He tended the garden, split wood for the cookstove, and raised goats as a hobby. Laura's books earned enough money so that it was no longer necessary to farm Rocky Ridge.

There were no horses left on Rocky Ridge

Farm. Manly drove a shiny new Chrysler instead. But Laura and Manly never stopped missing the days of horses and buggies.

Laura and Manly were always a little homesick for prairie country, so in 1938 they drove to South Dakota to visit their old friends and relatives. They were surprised to see that De Smet was a pretty little modern town instead of the pioneer settlement they remembered. Pa and Ma and Mary had died, but Grace lived nearby with her husband. After they visited with Grace, Laura and Manly drove farther west to visit Carrie in the Black Hills of South Dakota.

At home on Rocky Ridge, Laura was constantly busy with the writing of her books. In 1939 *By the Shores of Silver Lake* appeared. It told of Laura's family's move to Dakota Territory. In 1940 *The Long Winter* was published. In that book, Laura wrote of the blizzard winter of 1880–81, and how the Ingalls family and the Wilder boys survived it.

When describing children's letters to her, Laura told Rose they "all seem wildly interested

and want to know how, when and where Laura met Almanzo and about their getting married." She included the story of her first buggy ride with Manly in *Little Town on the Prairie*, which was published just before America entered World War II in 1941.

In 1943 *These Happy Golden Years*, the story of Laura's teaching and her happy wedding, was published. Laura was seventy-six when she completed her eighth book. Although the letters continued to pour in, asking for more tales of Laura and Almanzo, Laura was finished.

But Laura could hardly stop writing, because every day as many as fifty letters arrived from readers. Laura answered each one. A fourth-grade class wrote, hoping that the Little House stories were true. Laura replied: "You ask if Laura was a real person. She was. I was the Laura you have been reading about. The books are true stories about me and my parents and sisters. Things happened to them just as I have told in the books."

Children wanted to know what became of

the characters Laura had written of. She wrote, "Pa and Ma lived for a while on their homestead and then moved into town, where Pa did carpentry. After Mary graduated from the College for the Blind, she lived at home. She was always cheerful and busy with her work, her books, and music. Carrie worked for *The De Smet News* for a while after finishing high school, and then she married a mine owner and moved to the Black Hills. Grace married a farmer and lived a few miles outside of De Smet."

Laura sent Pa's fiddle back to South Dakota to be displayed in the museum near the state capitol building in Pierre. She enjoyed getting letters from children who saw the fiddle and went on to see where she had lived in De Smet. People who recalled Laura's family gladly showed visitors where Pa's homestead was, and they pointed out old buildings on Main Street that Laura had described in her books.

The Little House books were so popular that Harper & Brothers decided to publish new editions with illustrations by Garth Williams. In

1947 he arrived at Rocky Ridge to meet Laura and Almanzo. He studied their old photographs and visited the sites of the books. It took six years to complete his illustrations.

In 1949 Laura received a great honor. A library in Detroit, Michigan, was named for her. She and Manly were proud and pleased. But later that year ninety-two-year old Manly became ill. On October 23, 1949, Manly died at Rocky Ridge. He and Laura had been married for sixty-four years. Laura continued to live on the farm she and Manly had built. Although she missed Manly, her life was full of happy memories.

The letters still came, full of love for Laura and her books. When Laura turned eighty-four in 1951, nearly a thousand birthday cards were delivered to her. Children came knocking at Laura's door, shyly asking to meet her. "I cannot bear to disappoint a child," Laura said. She autographed their books, showed them through her home, and told them about Almanzo, Mary, Pa and Ma, and other people from her stories.

The children of Mansfield loved Laura's books too. They knew their favorite author lived in the white house on the hill a mile from town. They saw her in church and walking down the street in Mansfield when she did her errands.

Down the road from Laura's house lived two young boys who became Laura's faithful friends. They brought her mail, helped her with chores, and spent hours just visiting her. The boys often sat wide-eyed as Laura told them stories, just as Pa had once done. At Christmastime Laura gave them copies of her books. She loved them, just as she loved all the children around the world who read her books.

And children everywhere loved her back.

Afterword

LAURA INGALLS WILDER lived on happily at Rocky Ridge Farm. On February 10, 1957, three days after her ninetieth birthday, she died. After Laura's death her friends and neighbors met with Rose and asked her to preserve Rocky Ridge as a memorial for Little House readers to visit. The Laura Ingalls Wilder Home and Museum was founded, and later each of Laura's homesites was restored. Every year thousands of people from all over the world visit.

Rose continued to be a busy author after Laura

Laura Ingalls Wilder

died. In addition to her own books, Rose contributed to *On the Way Home*, published in 1962. It included Laura's diary of her last coveredwagon trip and Rose's memories of the first years on Rocky Ridge.

Rose inherited her family's love of travel. When she was eighty-one, she planned a trip around the world. Before she left, however, Rose died suddenly on October 30, 1968. She was the last descendant of Pa and Ma Ingalls.

An unpublished manuscript in Laura's handwriting was found in her home. *The First Four Years* was published in 1971, and it told about the early years of Laura and Almanzo's marriage.

In the 1970s a television series based on the Little House books was created. *Little House on the Prairie* was one of television's most popular shows for many years. It is still shown around the world in many languages. *West from Home*, a collection of Laura's letters to Almanzo from her 1915 trip to San Francisco to visit Rose, was published in 1974.

AFTERWORD

Laura's books have been translated into seventeen languages and have been read by millions of people. She remains one of the world's best-loved authors.